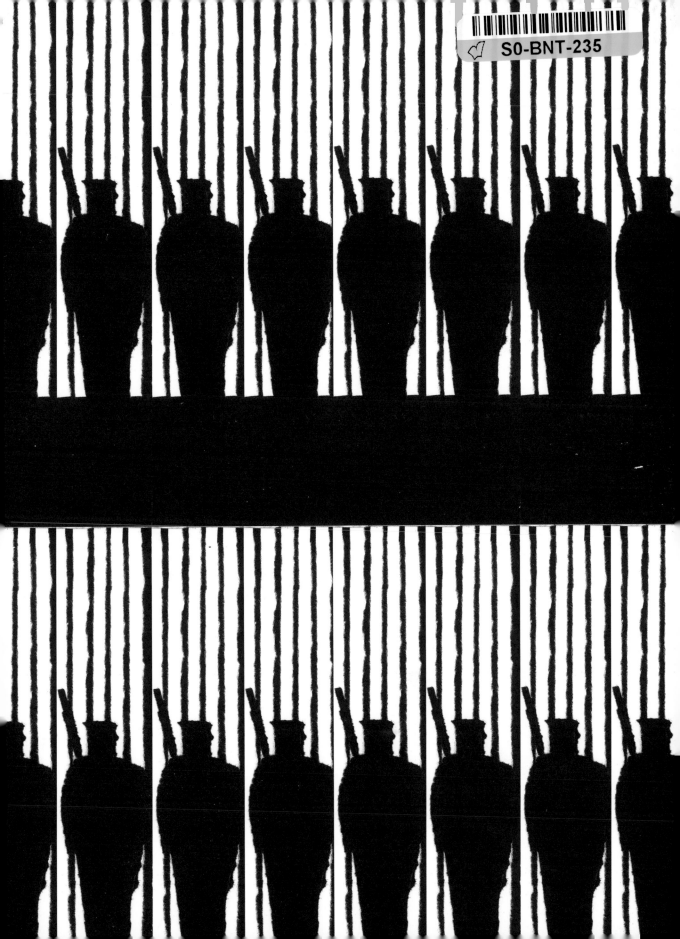

Revolution
First published in France under the title *Révolution*
© 2003 Editions du Seuil

First English edition copyright © 2008 Tara Books

Text and illustrations: Sara

Cover Design: Avinash Veeraraghavan

Production: C. Arumugam

ISBN: 978-81-86211-46-5

Published in association with the French Embassy in India.

Publisher's Note

French Focus is a new series of visual arts titles published by Tara Books in association with the French Embassy in India. Some of the most daring and creative visual books being published today come from France, and over the years, Tara's books have found homes with some of the finest French publishers. We hope to reciprocate with this series, and introduce readers to our favourites – from art books for adults to picture books for children, or indeed books that straddle genres and can only be described as 'Beaux Livres' or 'Beautiful Books'.

We are proud to start the series with *Revolution* by Sara. We have long respected Sara's talents as an illustrator, and nothing could be more historically French than its subject matter.

Revolution

Sara

TARA BOOKS

Oooooh!

The tanks!

Prisoner!

Farewell, little flag!

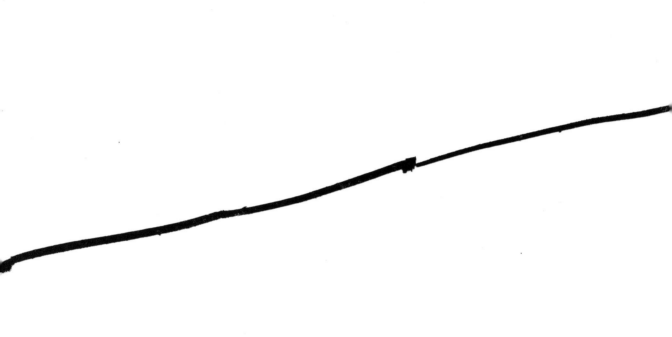

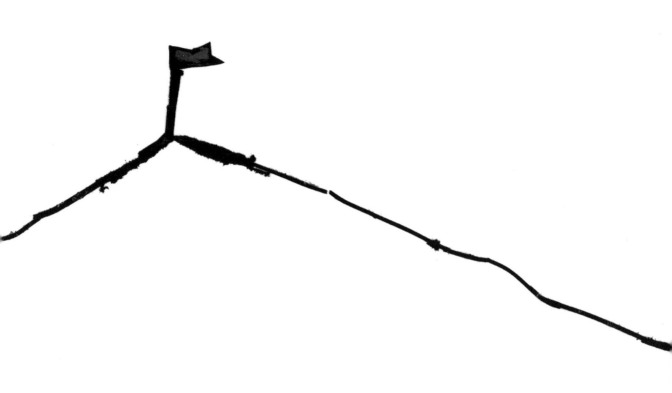

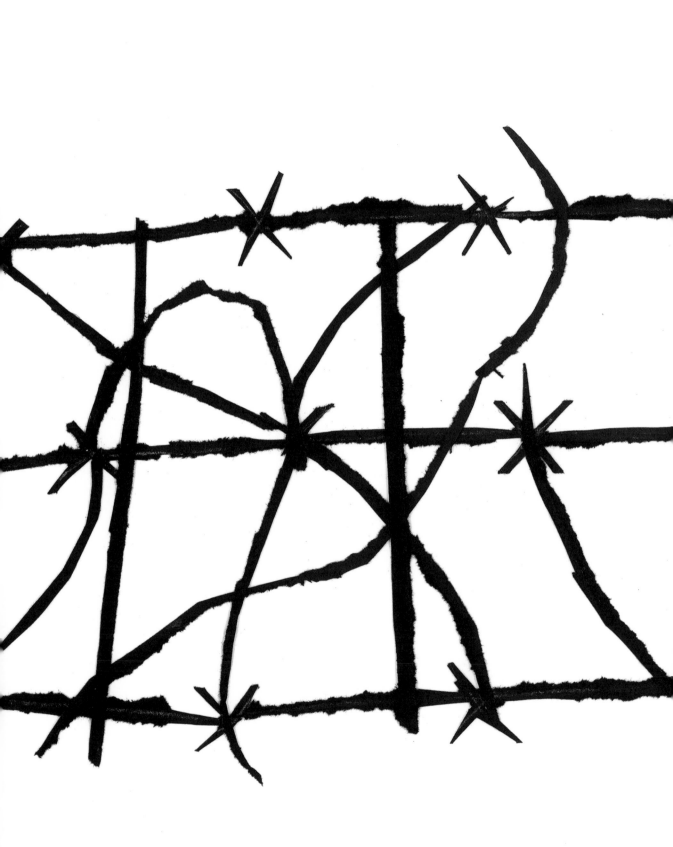

Must escape!

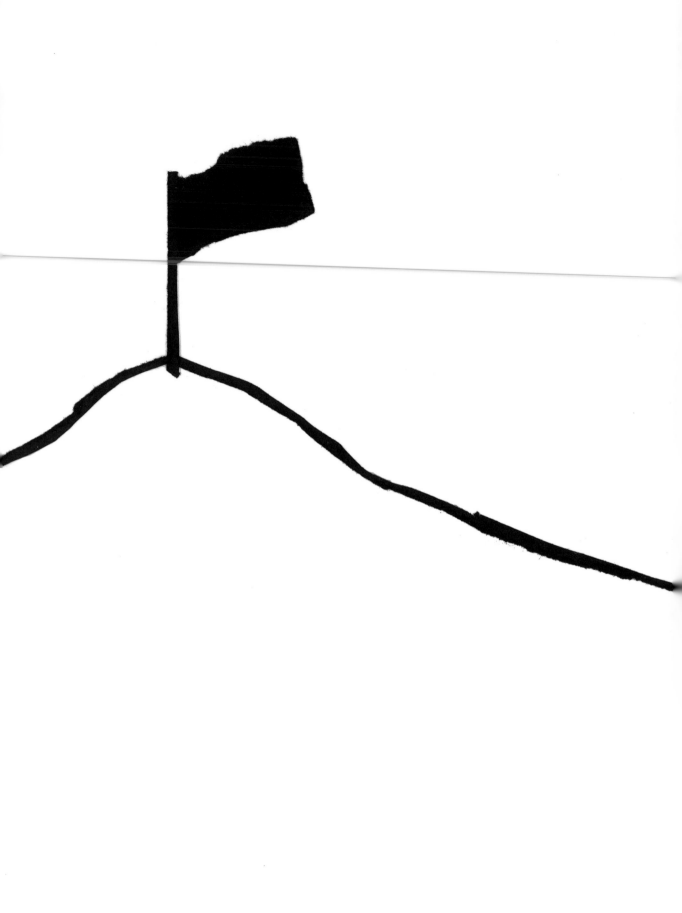

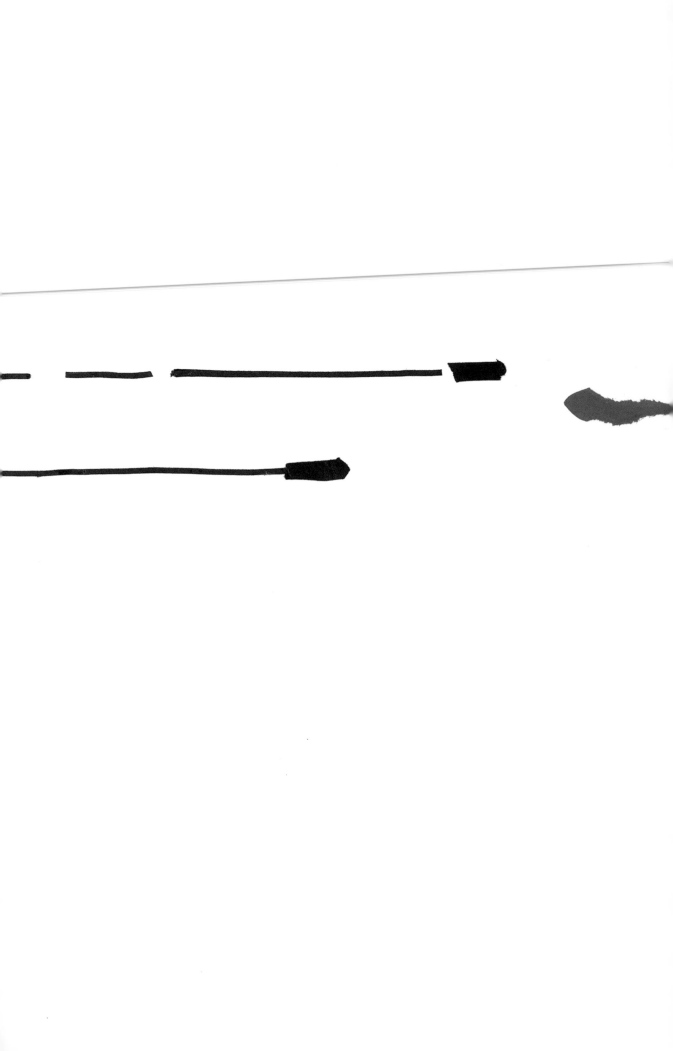

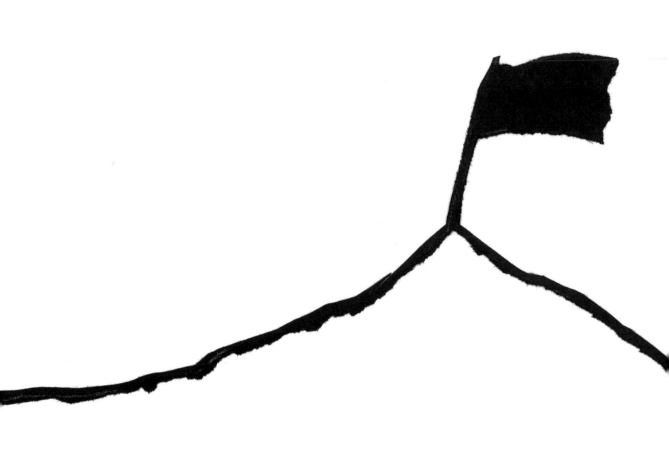

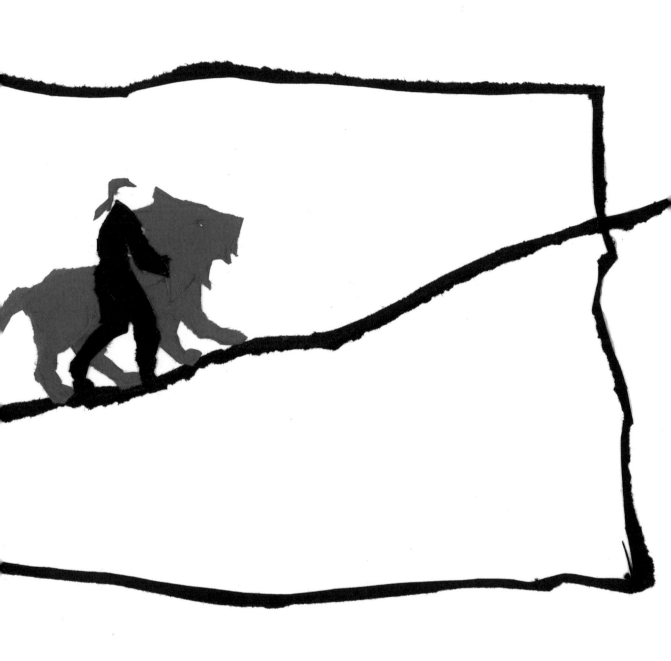

Revolution and Memory

As a graphic fable, *Revolution* invokes and celebrates what Fidel Castro once described as an ancient right of rebellion against tyranny. But the fable is also an inexorably modern one, featuring as its central character a red-scarved citizen, possessed of an implacable will to liberty. The citizen is up against the menacing power of a state or class, which hides behind barbed wire and bayonets. A solitary red flag affirms her defiance, guides her resistance and enshrines her impending martyrdom.

Revolution draws out a terse tale: it does not tell you about what happens after, whether the revolting citizen, along with others, form a new state, and a new ruling class; whether the red-scarves deal justly with their former oppressors and thus sustain their vision of the good society. Neither does it tell you what brings about the revolution. Rather it concentrates on that moment of confrontation between liberty and tyranny, which ends in triumph and sacrifice–a moment celebrated by revolutionary memory the world over. The heroic resister who fights power and goes down fighting is the ideal icon whose martyrdom represents both a historical swipe at a hated and unjust old order and an anticipation of utopia.

Walter Benjamin described the iconic significance of revolutions in memorable terms. He noted that revolutions are triggered off by the memory of enslaved grandfathers and not just the prospect of liberated children. He held that the revolutionary moment–captured in the artist Paul Klee's *Angelus Novus*, the departing Angel of History–is inexorable and ruptural. Just violence is informed by memory, yet it annihilates the old world because it is past its time. In an act of articulate vandalism, an irate revolutionary in France actually shot at the clock in the royal palace which, until then, had commanded human and historical time.

Another sense of revolution is encoded in Mao Zedong's cryptic response to what he thought of the French revolution: it was too early to say! He was referring to not merely the uniqueness of the event, but also the infinite and durable possibilities which the act of revolting against class and state encapsulates. For it is not only the event itself, but also how it is remembered, renewed, anticipated and re-made in each historical instance.

This double sense of the revolution, as an event that upturns the world and whose effects are to be forever anticipated is clearly millenarian–this is clear from the responses of those who bore witness to its happening, either because they were part of it, or alive when it happened. William Wordsworth's early verse, when he was still enraptured with the French revolution, is of this kind: 'Bliss was it in that dawn to be alive, but to be young was very heaven'. Alexander Blok's *The Twelve* conjures up an unforgettable image of the Bolsheviks in 1917 Moscow: 'they march with sovereign tread … carrying a blood-red flag...' and ahead of them goes Jesus Christ, a 'flowery diadem of frost' on his head. John Reed described the events that led to the fall of the Czar and the creation of the first socialist state as the 'ten days that shook the world'.

Millenarianism was not merely what poets fancied–it also made for radical politics. Olympe de Gouges who issued *The Declaration of the Rights of Women* in the wake of the French Revolution, noted that women now had the authority and legitimacy to question and displace the 'perpetual tyranny of man'. For Touissant de L'Ouverture in Haiti in the 1790s, the French revolution, especially the *Declaration of the Rights of Man and of the Citizen* that it brought forth, was a tocsin that would sound the death knell of race hatred and slavery in that French colony.

It is revolutionary hope which moves the pages of this book as well. Passed down, inherited and re-made in song, text and art, it exists here and elsewhere as the very stuff of memory.

***

Rather than the actual sequence of historical events in any given instance, it is revolutionary memory that has inspired resisters to protest and overthrow tyranny in their own contexts, which were often widely different from those in which the earliest modern revolutions took place.

National liberation struggles and struggles in the mid-twentieth century and after, against collusive local rulers and their colonial masters in much of Africa, Latin America and Asia took inspiration from the revolutions of the past. Algeria, Mozambique, Angola and the triumph of Vietnam immediately come to mind. The Cuban revolution, and its apostolic power, so memorably associated with Che Guevara, the

Sandinista hour in Nicaragua, the much mangled revolution in El Salvador, the repeated calls to strike at the barricades that had convulsed the streets of Chile and Argentina, the revolutions that never were, but which left behind inspiring poignant memories, as in parts of India, Indonesia and the Philippines: in these varied contexts, revolutionary memory, as much as the bind of historical conditions incited action on the streets. Revolutionary memory kept hope alive in the harshest of conditions, as in pre-apartheid South Africa, in Pahlavi-ruled Iran, and in what was once imperial Nepal.

In places where social and economic injustice have dehumanised millions of lives, leaders and ideologues drew on the memory archive of past revolutions, even when they did not wish to fight in exactly the same manner. For, Dr B. R. Ambedkar, the great pacifist anti-caste leader from India, the famed watchwords of the French revolution–liberty, equality and fraternity –proved immensely inspiring in the relentless struggle he waged against the indecent heirarchies of caste, and the relegation of an entire class of people to 'untouchable' status. Men like him rendered the language of revolution resonant with the cry of peace and justice–a resonance that is also heard in Martin Luther King's valiant politics against race and inequality in the United States of America. For Ambedkar and King, to revolt meant to re-make ethical life as well. For Dr Ambedkar the Buddha was the ideal revolutionary; for King, Christ was a spiritual rebel.

Women's movements and groups across the world have always found the revolutionary moment fascinating, for what it could shatter and what it could not. Women that took part in the French revolution wondered what shooting at the clock actually meant for them. Was it an indicaton that a new hour was dawning or were they to be returned to the kitchen once the revolution was off the streets and male revolutionaries were in charge of the state? The Bolshevik Alexandra Kollantai argued that women's rights to sexual autonomy and reproductive choice had to be made part of the socialist project, even if socialist men did not think so. Feminists in Latin America, and elsewhere, were beset by a 'gathering rage' in the wake of the revolutions in their contexts, since they felt that a largely male radical leadership was not willing to undertake the sort of fundamental changes in gender relations that they sought.

For some feminists, revolution has not been so much the one decisive moment, but the moment renewed in a spirit of permanent protest against injustices that won't go away. The women of Greenham Common in the United Kingdom protested the manufacture of nuclear arms for over two decades, starting in 1981. A similar spirit has enabled women from warring sides to come together and protest war and violence in places as far apart as Ireland, Palestine and Sri Lanka.

Even when critically examined and rejected, revolutionary memory compels reluctant admiration. Mahatma Gandhi admired the virtues of socialism and was captivated by what the moment could accomplish. But he was not impressed by the methods used by the revolutionaries.

The Zapatistas in Chiapas, Mexico are both critics and fellow travellers with the spirit of past revolutions. Their struggle for justice which began in the early 1990s is waged as if revolution was a permanent state of existence. Memory is central to their struggle, but they are not merely haunted by the phantoms of enslaved grandfathers. Rather they wish to recall into the present what has been lost in this suffering and enslavement. As a Zapatista woman revolutionary put it, 'we teach our children our language to keep alive our grandmothers'. Also, for the Zapatistas, a revolution does not break with time, neither is time linear. Rather they understand time to move spirally. Their revolution thus moves away from the savage and alienating effects of industrial capitalism, and inwards towards new words and thoughts as well as an older, more humane and responsible sense of the universe.

This book gestures towards diverse histories and events, but the power of what it represents is not exhausted by any of them. The red lion in the flag continues to beckon towards the future, even as it recalls past resistance and martyrdom.

V. Geetha
Tara Books

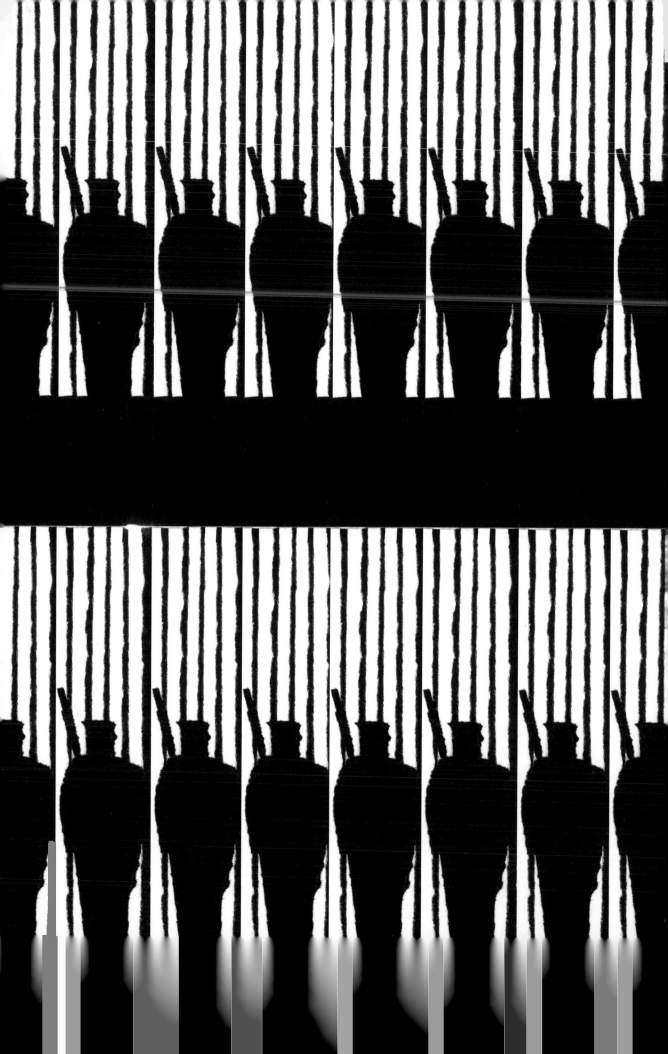